I0209938

Healing Depression

Ultimate Guide On What Turns Depression On And What

Turns It Off

William M. Curtis

Table of Contents

Copyright © 2019 by William M. Curtis

All rights reserved. No part of this publication may be reproduced, distributed, or transmitted in any form or by any means, including photocopying, recording, or other electronic or mechanical methods, without the prior written permission of the publisher, except in the case of brief quotations embodied in critical reviews and certain other non-commercial uses permitted by copyright law.

INTRODUCTION

Tired of suffering from been depressed? This fast, easy read is an excellent guide if you want to feel healthful and happy. During the past decade, depression rates has skyrocketed, and one in four of people around the globe have problems with major depression at some point within their lives. Naturally hundreds of thousands of people are influenced by depression each year, which can result in problems with work, relationships, home existence and physical health. Right now tell me where have we gone wrong?

This book will guide you on all the steps you need to take and what you have to do, to say goodbye to depression in your life.

CHAPTER 1

Diabetes and Depression

Managing Your Mental Wellness Along With Type 1 or Type 2 Diabetes.

Controlling type 1 or type 2 diabetes, chronic autoimmune diseases, could be highly challenging because of setbacks and several challenges on the way. The continuous vigilance necessary to manage blood sugars, navigate healthcare services, medication side effects, and various other related health issues can lead to an elevated risk of major depression. Left untreated, melancholy can lead to poor lifestyle options that worsen physical wellness.

In case you have diabetes, or somebody you like does, it's vital that you be aware of the chance of developing depression. Experts have found that both conditions occur doubly frequently as you'll predict predicated on chance, and therefore diabetes and despair affect each other in a few ways. The partnership between type 2 diabetes and depressive disorder is bidirectional, and therefore each can place a person at risk for the other. If one has depression, they are in a higher threat of leading a sedentary way of life and eating foodstuffs that are sugary or fatty, that may result in type 2 diabetes. If indeed they currently have type 2 diabetes, the burnout that may come with controlling the disease, can result in depression. Meanwhile, people who have type 1 diabetes-which isn't due to diet or lifestyle elements, but rather due to a pancreas that cannot produce insulin-can also be extremely challenging to control, which places one at risk for developing depressive symptoms. Once depressive symptoms develop, it could become increasingly hard to control diabetes and can result in physical problems and decreased life span.

If you're uncertain whether you may be experiencing depression, you can search for these signs:

- Insufficient interest in activities

- Depressed mood or irritability

- Changes in sleep patterns

- Changes in appetite

- Emotions of guilt or despair

- Lack of energy

- Trouble concentrating

- Suicidal thoughts

Risk Factors Connected with Diabetes and Depression

There are numerous environmental factors that may affect the chance of developing both conditions. These range from:

- Poverty

- Childhood adversity

- Poor social environments

- Lower physical activity

- Maternal stress just before birth

It isn't known whether taking antidepressant medication places a person at risk for diabetes, but associations have been observed between the two. Invest the antidepressants or are thinking about them, speak to your doctor about the dangers of weight adjustments and hyperglycemic and hypoglycemic results that can place you at risk for developing type 2 diabetes.

Researchers likewise have found that individuals with type 2 diabetes who make use of insulin are in higher risk for developing unhappiness in comparison to people that take non-insulin medicines or only change diet or lifestyle practices. This is because these folks may experience additional tension in handling the diabetes and accessing healthcare services.

For those who have diabetes, make sure to tell your physician if you begin to note that you're losing curiosity in things you once found pleasurable or you have emotions of hopelessness or a lesser mood. Speak to them in case you have a history of depressive disorder in your loved ones or find the difficulties of controlling your diabetes to become tiring.

Treatment Options

Common interventions for depression include cognitive behavioral therapy, which helps people right dangerous thought patterns and behaviors that may increase depressive symptoms, and also interventions such as organized problem solving, motivational interviewing, and interpersonal and psychodynamic approaches.

Medication also may help with lifting feeling and managing symptoms.

Treatment plans for diabetes furthermore to standard health care can include behavioral self-management applications that help people boost healthy behaviors and improve control more than their blood glucose. Both diabetes and major depression may improve with concentrate on lifestyle adjustments, such as enhancing diet and exercising frequently.

Many patients could find that having treatment groups communicate and collaborate with one another (nurse practitioner, diabetes educator, doctor, psychologist, counselor etc.) may prove useful in addressing the problems unique to people that have both conditions.

If you're uncertain where to start, speak to your doctor

about your family's medical and psychiatric plus your own concerns. Build relationships diabetes educators about healthful habits that lower threat of melancholy and don't hesitate to require a referral to a counselor or psychologist in your town. If you have despair and are worried about developing diabetes, you might want to speak to your doctor about creating a collaborative team to handle risk elements and how antidepressant medicines may potentially influence physical wellness such as excess weight or blood sugar.

With the proper tools and the proper team, people who have type 1 or type 2 diabetes may lead emotionally and physically healthy lives, as can people that have depression. Consider today who you can recruit to assist you develop healthy life-style habits for your brain and body.

Coping with Sadness: How Will Sadness Change from Depression?

Sadness and depression talk about some traits but won't be the same. Understanding the difference can be important since clinical unhappiness requires treatment

Everyone includes a bad day right now and again-a painful argument with a partner, the increased loss of a much loved pet, getting passed more than for an advertising, and other everyday disappointments-can make you feel awful. Sadness is certainly a standard emotion that should fade over time however when that melancholy isn't short-term, the danger of depressive disorder may be coming.

"Sadness is a standard human being emotion that everyone feels every once in a while." "It is associated with a hard life event like a loss of someone you care about, a breakup or additional hurtful event that outcomes within an untoward outcome. Whenever a person feels unfortunate, sadness is usually the dominant emotion. But there may be intervals of levity and much less severe mood. Sadness may also occasionally end up being relieved by venting, crying, exercising or various other ways of releasing emotion."

Sadness varies in strength and duration, but a defining feature is that it's a short-term feeling. "Ultimately, it fades and eventually resolves. If sadness proceeds to intensify, will not ultimately fade or lasts for an extended period, you should look for support from a mental doctor because major depression is a chance."

CHAPTER 2

What's the Difference Between Sadness and Depression?

When sadness is persistent and won't leave, that's when major depression begins to reel its ugly mind. "Unlike sadness, depression isn't common." "Impacting a lot more than 16 million adults in America, depression is a significant medical illness that inhibits what sort of person thinks, feels and functions, and may cause persistent sadness. People that have depression frequently have hopelessness and an inability to see enjoyment paired with physical symptoms, such as for example changes in rest, energy, appetite and capability to concentrate."

Depressive disorder is a diagnosable emotional health that may include emotions of sadness, but also contains other symptoms that can be found simultaneously. "These symptoms can include diminished interest or satisfaction in activities, adjustments in sleeping and consuming patterns, agitation, exhaustion, inability to concentrate, emotions of worthlessness or guilt and recurring thoughts of loss of life."

Depression could be triggered by exterior circumstances or could be because of physiological pre-disposition. The word "depressed" is frequently misused and self-reported as a sense unto itself, as in, "Personally i think depressed." Clinical depression, nevertheless, can only become diagnosed by a mental doctor that can evaluate symptoms and recommend right treatment.

Symptoms of Depression

There are particular cardinal top features of depression,

such as:

- Feeling depressed during the day of all or all days

- Too little interest and enjoyment in activities you utilized to find pleasurable

- Having difficulty sleeping, or sometimes sleeping too much

- Trouble eating, including eating an excessive amount of, or even inadequate, which can lead to undesirable weight gain or loss

- A sense of restlessness, irritability or agitation during the day

- Extreme fatigue and lack of energy

- Unwanted or exaggerated emotions of guilt or worthlessness

The shortcoming to concentrate or even to even make rational decisions

Thoughts of suicide, or thinking frequently about loss of life and dying

Treatment Differences

Sadness may weigh you down even though you're experiencing it, in fact it is important to focus on how you're feeling. You can stabilize your mental wellness by keeping a positive outlook, encircling yourself with a solid support network, eating healthful and exercising, though period is often the easiest way to overcome sadness.

"In the event that you or someone you like is experiencing symptoms of melancholy, motivate them to get screened and talk to their doctor." "It really is okay to require help and to use your physician to customize a highly effective treatment plan that will help your business lead a happier, healthier lifestyle. A common treatment for despair includes the mixture of antidepressant medication and psychotherapy or 'chat therapy.' Nevertheless, a startling 5.5 million depression sufferers in America do not reap the benefits of antidepressants."

Antidepressants usually do not work immediately and usually need an amount of adjustment. For treatment-resistant depression among the newer treatment plans is a number of ketamine infusions. If a person's depression is serious and a healthcare group deems the individual to be a risk to himself, the individual could be admitted to a medical center where they could be noticed and treated. Outpatient services and clinics are additional options.

Most of us experience those occasions in life where in

fact the fact presented is significantly less than our anticipations, whether it's not receiving the positioning, the romantic relationship, or the knowledge we felt would make you feel happy. "As we metal ourselves against the unavoidable realities of existence and try, and try once again, we find that sadness starts to wane and we effectively recover our feeling of wellbeing, finding that sadness isn't just a normal emotional condition, but that it's transitory." "Whenever we consider the significant variations between sadness and unhappiness, the critical elements we observe will be the intensity and duration of the symptoms. Will be the symptoms you feel chronic, continuous, pervasive, and disruptive to your daily life?"

You'll be able to overcome sadness and depressive disorder, once we know how our brains function. "We are coping with two unique, emotionally-charged encounters." "What we realize is that whenever people switch their thought procedures, and challenge just how their brains talk with them, they have an excellent opportunity to undermine the energy that sadness and major depression have over them. After you have fulfilled sadness and depression, they'll be around everyone once in a while."

Developing Self-Esteem: 5 Techniques to improve How You See Yourself

Everyone encounters bouts of self-question, but if low self-esteem has effects on your daily life, try these 5 tactics to build self-confidence and increase your self-esteem

Your sense of self-well worth will impact every arena you will ever have. Your task, your relationships, and actually your physical and mental wellness are reflection of your self-esteem. But what precisely helps shape your look as of yourself as well as your abilities? The simple truth is that your degree of self-esteem may have become or shrunk based about how folks have treated you previously and the evaluations you've produced about your daily life and your choices.

The good thing is that you possess a good amount of control with regards to increasing your degree of self-worth. There are basic, concrete changes you may make that challenge your brain and your body. One particular change is to do something to lessen negative thinking and build-up positive, encouraging thoughts about the individual you are and will be.

CHAPTER 2

Replace Bad With Positive Thinking

Identify triggers - To boost the level of positive considering in your day-to-day lifestyle, you first need to recognize what people, places, and points promote negative thinking. Probably it's the total amount in your money, or simply it's a coworker who's usually complaining. You can't modify certain situations, nevertheless, you can transform how you respond to them and understand them. That starts with watching what makes you feel sad or anxious.

Take down notes - There's a continuing dialogue, or "self-talk," usually happening in the human brain as you start your entire day. This self-talk consumes the globe around you and makes evaluations about yourself and others. So make an effort to begin noticing any interesting styles in this dialogue. Is usually this thinking predicated on facts? Or could it be generally leaning towards the irrational, always assuming the most severe in a situation?

Challenge your thinking - If you see your self jumping to conclusions, or constantly downplaying the positive about yourself, you then have to intensify and then add positive considering to your self-talk. Understanding how to concentrate on the positive and also to encourage yourself is like a strengthening a muscle mass. You have to exercise your brain thoroughly just a little every day time to develop a convenience of positive considering, to forgive yourself when you make errors, and to figure out how to provide yourself credit when you accomplish an objective.

Take an Inventory

If you're uncertain where you rank with regards to self-esteem, taking a listing of your individual qualities can help. When you are listing even more weaknesses than strengths, this could be an indicator that you have a tendency to be too much on yourself. Think about what talents, capabilities, and passions you possess not listed and maybe even discovered yet. By no means assume you understand everything about yourself and what you're with the capacity of. People who have high self-esteem leave space for self-discovery each day.

Acknowledge Successes

Often people who have low self-esteem will dismiss their successes as luck or prospect. Or they might concentrate on not being ideal rather than highlighting what lengths they have arrive. People who have high self-esteem take time to celebrate their accomplishments. They state,

"Many thanks," when people compliment them, instead of dismissing their compliment. This doesn't mean that individuals with high-personal esteem are arrogant or narcissistic; they just trust their skills and acknowledge successes if they do happen.

Stop Comparing Yourself

Other people can't be typical with regards to your self-esteem. It is because you'll constantly find a person who appears much better than you or even more able than you in virtually any arena of existence. Social press certainly doesn't help, as experts have found that individuals who check social mass media very frequently will have problems with low self-esteem. Remind yourself that individual's usually only talk about the best elements of their life on-line. Your own life ought to be the yardstick instead of others' lives because what's your best might not be somebody else's, and vice versa. Remind yourself that if you make a noticeable difference or prevent yourself from repeating a blunder, you are making improvement.

Practice Self-Care

The more you prove that you value your wellbeing, the more you create a capacity for loving other areas of yourself. Pay attention to your body and prevent foods that make you feel irritable or tired. Consuming healthy and exercising can also boost positive thinking and assist you to feel even more encouraged about your own future. In the event whereby you spend time with people who care about you, you might find that all of a sudden it's easier that you should look after yourself.

Understand that learning positive thinking and developing healthy way of living strategies aren't likely to end up being overnight miracles. Becoming kind to yourself and upping your feeling of self-worth does take time, practice, and persistence. But the even more you challenge your ideas and perspectives, the higher joy you could find in yourself as well as your capabilities. You'll feel pleased with how far you've arrive, and you'll anticipate the future.

CHAPTER 3

6 Things Never to Tell a Person With Depression

Major depressive disorder (also known as "depression") is common but serious disposition disorder. Depressive disorder causes symptoms that negatively affect what people thinks, seems, and copes with day to day activities such as for example eating, sleeping, or operating.

Depression is seen as a persistent design of sadness (or irritability in kids) or insufficient pleasure in most actions most of your day, nearly each day, for at least fourteen days. Depression range from a wide variety of symptoms (rather than everyone encounters every symptom), including:

- Sad, anxious, or empty mood

- Emotions of hopelessness

- Emotions of guilt or worthlessness

- Irritability

- Lack of interest or enjoyment in activities

- Changes in feeding on patterns, including weight reduction or weight gain

- Fatigue

- Moving or talking slowly

- Restlessness

- Difficulty concentrating or taking decisions

- Rest disturbance (difficulty falling or staying asleep or oversleeping)

- Thoughts of loss of life or suicide, including suicide attempts

Physical pains or digestive issues with zero known medical cause (including frequent headaches, muscle cramps, or various other pain)

Based on the National Institute of Mental Wellness, depression is among the mostly diagnosed mental disorders in the US and can be related to a mixture of genetic, biological, environmental, and psychological factors.

If you have a pal or family member fighting depression, you will possibly not know what to state or how exactly to lend support. The one best thing that you can do for a pal with depression is pay attention without judgment.

There are a variety of phrases that are occasionally used in combination with good intentions but can in fact make a person with depression feel worse. Avoid these phrases when assisting a pal with depression: ***"Don't consider it"***

Some individuals with depression actually have problems

with rumination. Ruminating means repetitively exceeding a thought or issue without completion, and it could contribute to increased emotions of worthlessness or helplessness in depressed sufferers.

You can't simply set depression aside, and tell a person to avoid considering their problems which can trigger them to activate rumination. One research discovered that although ruminators perform tend to touch base for help, they often times don't obtain the support they look for and their rumination causes interpersonal friction. Whenever a support program pulls apart or tells the depressed person to avoid great deal of thought, the ruminator has even more to ruminate about.

"Think positive!"

Although psychotherapists often use cognitive reframing to greatly help depressed individuals replace mental poison with positive ones, this technique does take time and helps the individual explore the roots of the unfavorable thought cycle.

Informing a depressed person to "think positive" is normally dismissive of the condition that triggers the symptoms and spots blame on the individual struggling with the condition.

"I find out how you are feeling"

Although this statement is empathic and designed to help the depressed person experience understood, it could backfire. There exists a factor between clinical melancholy and sadness. It's regular to experience emotions of sadness, but melancholy is a feeling disorder that negatively impacts a person's capability to attend to regular daily activities.

Statements like this one minimize the person's discomfort

"Count your blessings"

There is commonly a whole lot of guilt and shame with despair. Depressed people frequently describe emotions of guilt, worthlessness, and helplessness. Because depression can be an invisible disease (people do not necessary appear "depressed"), there exists a stigma surrounding the condition.

Statements like "count your blessings" or "be thankful for what you have got" imply that the individual is depressed because he or she simply can't see what they carry out have.

"It may be worse"

Comparisons to other folks fighting other battles are rarely useful. Whenever a depressed person gets to out for sociable support, they're searching for empathy and compassion.

Although there may be other people experiencing any number of medical ailments, telling a depressed person what other people has is worse only to make you see yourself and feel ashamed.

"Get over it"

Depression is a significant medical condition, and telling you to definitely move on or overcome it won't actually remedy it. This type of declaration lacks compassion and can likely make the individual with depression experience shamed and misunderstood.

There are no perfect answers with regards to supporting a pal or cherished one with depression, and questions could be simply as helpful as statements whenever a depressed person opens up. Get one of these handful of these empathic responses:

- How can I assist you to in this difficult time?

- I'm sorry that you're getting hurt. I'm right here for you.

- Tell me more about it.

- Do you want to go for a walk with me?

- MAY I keep you organize today?

- Can I get you dinner this week?

- Thank you for sharing this with me to ensure that I can know very well what you're going through.

CHAPTER 4

Coping with a Depressed Person

Depression is much greater than a bad feeling. It's a problem that casts a shadow over a person's thoughts, emotions, perceptions of the globe, and their associations with others. This makes coping with anyone who is depressed quite a demanding job. Researchers estimate that nearly one from every five people in America will experience major depressive disorder at some point within their lifetime. So it's likely that you'll have someone you care about who has experienced the disorder at one stage or another.

Depressive disorder looks different for differing people, so get rid of those stock pictures of the crying one who can't escape bed. Though people might encounter this extreme sadness, others may experience irritable, anxious, or angry. That continuously irritated friend who can't concentrate or rest at night? He could actually be depressed. Additional signs to consider might include lack of interest in actions which were once fun, problems making decisions, adjustments in sleeping and consuming, lack of energy or sluggishness, sense guilty or hopeless, and actually suicidal thoughts.

In the event that you live with somebody with depression, like an intimate partner or a member of family, you'll encounter your own hurdles. These might consist of:

- Sense angry about the disorder

- Perceiving the depressed person because ungrateful or too needy

- Fear or stress in expressing your frustrations

- Feeling your relationship requirements are not met

- Feeling frustrated by insufficient participation in chores

The temptation there will be to tell your beloved ones to "appear on the bright side" or "snap from it." But would you state that to an actually injured person? Mental disease can be difficult to comprehend what it really is like unless you've experienced it yourself. We reside in a global where *5 SIMPLE ACTIONS* is usually touted as the perfect solution is to all problems. However the fact is that getting up and going to function when you're depressed isn't about carrying out a basic life hack, summoning the proper quantity of willpower, or bribing yourself. Motivating capture phrases should never be helpful, and will overtimes be fulfilled with hostility and irritability.

Don't end up being discouraged. Overcoming depression can be done and most likely for many individuals, but it's no basic task. So what's the possible thing to do for your beloved?

Communicate - Take time to communicate to your beloved. Reassure them that you realize that depressive disorder is a problem and not an individual failing. Tell them you don't believe they are poor, and you know they aren't choosing to feel just how they perform. If you're having difficulty reframing, imagine how you'll react if your partner had a damaged leg. Healing does take time, and you can't pressure it.

Involve them - Involve the individual just as much as you can easily in the decision-making course of action. So instead of saying, "You have to escape the house and proceed outside today," you could state, "I'd like to obtain outside today. Would you rather get a walk in the recreation area or go visit a movie?" If indeed they refuse, it's essential never to force them to accomplish anything. Instead, provide authentic praise for the tiny successes and prevent sarcasm.

Avoid accusatory speech - View your words and make an effort to use *"I-statement"* instead of accusatory *"You-statements."* There's a notable difference between "I worth your mental health insurance and need to see you accomplish your targets," in comparison to "You by no means perform anything for yourself." Pressing someone's buttons might feel great in the moment nonetheless it won't solve anything. It's likely that a depressed person has already been struggling with emotions of guilt and self-criticism.

Practice self-care - Never forget to care and pay attention to your brain, body, and other human relationships when a cherished one is struggling. Depressed individuals are often perceived as becoming self-centered, because all their concentrate and energy is swept up in coping with the disorder. Consequently you may want to turn to additional friends and family users for support and encouragement. Guidance or a support group is definitely an incredibly helpful source to find out more about major depression but also to understand positive coping abilities for yourself as well.

If you're not sure to start out, remind yourself never to lose hope. Almost all of people with melancholy will improve with treatment, however the process will need time, persistence, setbacks, and like. Encourage your beloved one's to obtain help today and look for methods to support yourself as well.

CHAPTER 5

The Father Effect: Depression, Addiction, and Denial

Does depression trigger addiction or could it be the other method around? Both of these mental health issues often present collectively, and it could be difficult to determine which to take care of first

It happens to the very best of us. When your life begin to experience some enjoyment at every instant of it. Then all of a sudden things start spinning uncontrollable and we question what happened. Where is our joy coming from? Why are we feeling in this manner? No matter where we was raised or visited school. No matter which kind of job we've or where we live. What counts is that life tossed us a curveball and points aren't turning out just how we thought they might. And before we realize it, we become depressed and seek out a dependence on cope with this feelings. Simultaneously, of program, we are totally in denial about everything.

Major depression, Addiction, and Denial-the "Father" effect-is something specialists agree is an ever-growing concern.

Avoiding Emotions

"Avoiding feelings, such as sadness, keeps all of us from processing the proceedings." "It keeps us from having the ability to accept and move forward from the event. Negative feelings are useful, specifically sadness. Sadness can improve your judgment and inspiration. Those that allow themselves to see sadness may use this emotion as a catalyst to drive them out of their safe place and do even more to begin to feel better. Actually, those who sees their sadness also display greater perseverance."

But not many people are equipped to cope with sadness or bad emotions, and that's where the road to addictions will start. "Depression and addiction frequently go together, but which came first is not always obvious." "Oftentimes, drugs or alcoholic beverages are considered for rest from the mental discomfort of despair. In others, unhappiness develops consequently of the psychological and physical damage carried out by addiction."

Addiction + Mental HEALTH ISSUES

According to the DRUG ABUSE and Mental Health Companies Administration (SAMSHA), right now there are around nine million adults which have mental wellness and drug abuse problems. Sadly, no more than 7% are receiving treatment for both circumstances. When drug abuse is coupled with depression, these circumstances have a tendency to amplify each other, causing unwanted effects to multiply. And if one disorder is definitely treated without the addiction, recovery becomes significantly less likely.

It is important to comprehend that feelings have several parts to them. "We can feel great or positive about something as basic to be greeted by our doggie when we get back." "It is pleasurable and therefore you want to do it again. Negative experiences, nevertheless, are considered 'poor,' and we arrive to think that these ought to be avoided. Actually, we are trained from an extremely young age in order to avoid negative feelings. How many occasions have we noticed our parents insist there can be 'nothing at all to cry about?' Regrettably, this drive in order to avoid bad feelings can result in drug or alcohol misuse or various other self-harming behavior."

CHAPTER 6

Understanding Emotional Coping Skills

Medical experts concur that many folks have excess baggage left from their childhood that impacts how they handle their feelings as adults. Listed below are simply a few types of how kids are trained to cope with their feelings:

Avoid bad feelings no matter what. Children should "bury any bad emotions," and when all that discomfort and sadness is held inside, it could slowly surface later on through additional behaviors, including anger, overeating, and difficulties in coping with peers.

Pass judgment about others. When a kid feels badly about themselves, for instance, rather than coping with their own concern, they often times find it is simpler to focus on somebody else's faults. A kid might experience self-conscience about the look of them and accept making fun of somebody else's appearance, rather than seeking out to definitely speak about how exactly they experience themselves.

Keep their views to themselves. If a kid isn't given the chance to share their personal sights when something happens, ultimately they will continue steadily to suppress how they really feel.

Danger of Suicide

To create matters worse, those people who are depressed and dealing with their emotions through alcohol or substance abuse will be in threat of committing suicide. "When drug abuse is coupled with depression, the chance of self-inflicted loss of life grows exponentially." "Even though the required treatment help is obtainable, people that have depression and addiction problems face extra struggles. Drugs and alcohol can obtain in the form of mental wellness treatment, and major depression is an integral predictor of relapse back again to substance use."

Additionally there is another complication: those fighting addiction are usually unaware also, they are dealing with depression. Quite simply, their addiction has completely bought out their lives.

"Anyone who has experienced a recently available struggle, challenge, or tragedy may feel compelled in order to avoid processing the negative feelings linked to the experience." "Where in fact the denial lies is certainly in the addict's perception. I've done a whole lot of timelines with people in early recovery, and generally, their depressive disorder was the consequence of excessive reduction and tension. The contributing elements being brain changes due to the drugs, along with the lack of jobs, relationships, wellness, and pride."

Facing complications early is key since depressive disorder makes a person more susceptible to developing addiction and vice versa. Dealing with each issue-as soon since it manifests-can assist in preventing one issue from turning out to be two. Change a negative experience, like a reduction or defeat, by visually "rewriting" the story. Just provide it a different ending-the positive one you'd wished for. This mental workout reframes the adversity so that you can see it as a chance for development and learning-not really as a mortal blow that ends a profession.

CHAPTER 7

Depression in Males: The Routine of

Toxic Masculinity

What's toxic masculinity and how does it donate to depression in men?

Among the reasons we became a therapist is my curiosity in helping people experiencing anxiety, sociable awkwardness, bipolar disorder, and depression. Through the years I've noticed that lots of men with depressive disorder have problems admitting they are depressed. They often times can't even verbalize that, "I am depressed." Regarding to Mental Wellness America, six million males suffer from depression. Study conducted by US Division of Health insurance and Human Services demonstrates depressive symptoms in males have improved from 4.3 to 5.7% nationwide. Grim numbers for several however the most worrisome facet of all is the truth that untreated major depression can result in anti-interpersonal behavior and suicide.

Does depression in guys really change from depression in ladies? Yes, men seem to see and cope with melancholy in various ways than females but it's vital that you consider the effect of societal ideals of masculinity on the variations. There's a simplistic view which may be partially rooted in reality: women get sad, males get mad. Various other male symptoms include: exhaustion, body pain, serious sleep disturbances, and erection dysfunction.

How Toxic Masculinity Hurts Men

In the American culture, and others, a lot of men have a problem expressing emotion because of toxic masculinity. Toxic masculinity identifies actions that discourage shows of emotion-various other than anger-in guys which also encourages behavior that may deem the male "dominant" in confirmed situation. Even while children, young males who express emotions are in comparison to girls in a poor context. Common responses to youthful males who become psychological include:

- Boys don't cry!

- Man up!

- Don't be such a baby!

- Don't cry just like a girl!

- Be considered a man-get over it!

- You throw such as a girl!

You've most likely heard these phrases fond of you or somebody around you. You likely have observed them in dialogue or in storylines on TV shows and films. And, you may become guilty of uttering them yourself.

Imagine being a small boy, crying over an agonizing damage or an emotional heartbreak that feels as though the finish of the globe, and being told to "guy up," rather than getting gently asked what's causing you to cry, how you are feeling about it, and everything you think that you can do about it.

When emotions are dismissed and gender-defining thinking is heard repeatedly, a person learns in order to avoid expressing their real emotions and starts to bottle up sadness. As time passes, such behavior can result in a dysfunctional psychological expression and ultimately, despair.

A Cycle of Melancholy in Males: Recognizing the Symptoms

Whenever a young boy matures after absorbing the negativity portrayed simply by others, they often times raise their own children-especially males- the same manner. Society dictates that males be raised to think that confidence, strength, achievement, and composure will be the core elements to be a guy, and anything "psychological" is normally girly or womanly, and really should consequently be stifled and overlooked. Because of this, symptoms of unhappiness in men frequently manifest differently than they do in women.

Signs or symptoms of depression in males include:

- Eating disorders

- Erectile dysfunction

- Fatigue

- Feeling unfortunate or angry inside but displaying rage and anger to seem masculine

- Struggling to perform daily chores

- Increased irritability

- Lack of concentration

- Lack of curiosity at the job and in family

- Lack of sleep

- Self-medication with street drugs

- Suicidal thoughts

Men raised in something that promotes traditional masculinity have complicated emotions towards their own feelings. Often, they try to shut them off or prevent them completely. I think that this is why men will use external solutions to cope with the inward turmoil and discomfort due to depression. Men often handle depressive disorder by over-working. In addition they self-medicate by embracing substances such as alcohol and drugs in an effort to avoid coping with depression and panic. Physiologist and physician Sigmund Freud, who's broadly regarded as the daddy of psychoanalysis, famously stated people repress from their mindful brain what they believe are shameful thoughts. Put simply, people bury what they are ashamed of.

Lastly, many men communicate their internal conflicts simply by directing anger at those around them, like their partners or children. What perform all of these exterior "coping" methods have as a common factor? None of these actually help guys cope with, or also encounter, what they are in fact struggling with.

Changing Our Look at of Men and Depression

Unfortunately, I've had many male clients relay unpleasant tales about the insensitive responses they received if they confided in someone they care about their struggles with major depression. Sadly, they weren't fulfilled with sympathy or encouragement. Rather, remarks such as, "What are you depressed about, are you on your own period?" are pretty typical.

Yes, the friend was joking and most likely trying to

create my client experience better, but of training course had the contrary effect. It's simple to understand why men frequently prefer to keep melancholy to themselves-concealed from their family and friends members.

We have to change how exactly we see depression in men; depression isn't linked to gender. No male or female chooses to live with despair. Traumatic events result in depression, and we have to accept this reality rather than dispiriting the issue and the sufferer.

YOUR SKILL

Below are a few tips that will help you build trust and motivate the men you like to become more comfortable sharing their emotions:

Avoid trivializing depression in men. Rather than stating, "Are you insane?" or "Why are you doing things as an emotionally-challenged person?" make use of empathy and offer support to your male family and friends who are depressed. Choosing the best words can be hard and stating them can experience awkward but being ready to pay attention, without judgment, is usually the best thing that can be done for a person who is usually depressed. Motivate them to talk about their feelings with you, so when they do, supply the moral support that they want rather than belittling them.

Change your anticipations and reactions. As a therapist, I've witnessed that men experiencing depression never talk about their emotions because they might be mocked. The truth is that whenever someone is experiencing depression, sharing their emotions and feelings is necessary to greatly help them cope with the issue. We have to be better close friends, better partners and become the support that males need.

Be part of the answer by sincerely encouraging men to greatly help them express feelings better. To greatly help men you need to help them eliminate their hesitation in posting their emotions. We should accept the actual fact that expressing emotion and crying are regular tendencies for everyone, no matter gender. Crying should not be associated with gender functions. Addressing and processing feelings is what human being are used to, and crying is usually a fundamental emotion.

Each person exists with original assets and challenges that affect how they grow and develop biologically, psychologically, and socially. Adult in the family and also adults in neighborhoods, colleges and the broader community, can facilitate to see your face moving toward development and advancement. Help them face dangers and difficulties by helping them accomplish a positive end result. We often make reference to overcoming adversity as advertising resilience.

We are able to change the style of masculinity by informing children that it's good for boys expressing and show emotion. Man role versions can practice what they preach by expressing affection and emotion: informing their children they like them; being comfy hugging them; displaying that it's alright to cry at wedding ceremonies, funerals, if they are hurt, etc. and talking about everyday feelings such as, "my trip to work was mind-boggling and I struggled with some low factors." Teaching boys how exactly to express their feelings adequately is as important to assisting them become emotionally expressive. These lessons could have a positive influence on their life later on.

It has been too much time, that people have lived with the original style of masculinity and in the event that you ask, Now could be a great period to change the way the culture perceives in emotional responses in men.

Depression is usually a life-long illness. Generally, long-term help could be had a need to stay well, which include keeping treatment and developing and facilitating an idea for when symptoms come back. Setbacks can occur to anyone actually if you've been feeling well for a long period. Many men and ladies who live with unhappiness figure out how to cope and are in a position to live fulfilling lives. Consider it one stage at the same time, one day at the same time. Your loved ones, friends, and treatment group are resources.

CHAPTER 8

Stress and Phobias: What exactly are Specific Phobias?

A particular phobia is a kind of anxiety disorder thought as an intense, irrational concern with or aversion to something. Everyone experiences fear every once in a while. Whether flying through turbulence, anticipating a go at the doctor's workplace, or coping with a violent storm, anxiousness is definitely a universal feeling that people all proceed through at some time in our lives.

However, in case you have a particular phobia, you likely knowledge a feeling of dread or panic when confronted with a specific scenario or object. A particular phobia is a kind of anxiety disorder thought as a great or irrational concern with or aversion to something. These irrational fears can hinder personal relationships, function, and school, and stop you from enjoying lifestyle.

Unlike Generalized PANIC (GAD), specific phobias can be found in a number of forms. They are cued when a person is usually confronted with a particular circumstance or object, or also anticipates being met with it. Actually though the problem or object poses little if any actual risk to the individual, they often times cannot control their dread towards it and can actively avoid it no matter what. Although people with particular phobias identify the irrationality of their fears, the very thought of these fears only is often plenty of to cause huge, debilitating anxiety.

While ordinary fears cause small anxiety and can become more easily overcome, particular phobias physically and/or psychologically impair the affected person to this overwhelming extent that it's disabling to their lifestyle.

Based on the DSM-5, prevalence prices are around 5% in children, 16% in 13- to 17-year-olds, and around 3%-5% in older people. Females are more often affected than males.

Types of Specific Phobia

Particular Phobias are categorized into 5 types:

- Pet Phobias (e.g., canines, snakes, or spiders)

- Environment Phobias (e.g., heights, storms, water)

- Blood-Injection-Damage Phobias (e.g., concern with seeing blood, getting a blood check or shot, watching TV shows that display surgical procedure)

- Situational Phobias (e.g., airplanes, elevators,

traveling, enclosed places)

- Additional Phobias (e.g., phobic avoidance of circumstances that may result in choking, vomiting, or contracting a sickness; in kids, avoidance of loud appears like balloons popping or costumed character types like clowns)

Causes of Phobias

In most cases, particular phobias develop in early childhood between your ages of 7 and 11, though it's possible for a phobia to build up at any age. Particular phobias could be caused by a number of different facets: going through a traumatic event (e.g. getting attacked by a doggie); observing others going right through a traumatic event (e.g. witnessing a vehicle accident); an unexpected anxiety attack (e.g. while flying within an airplane); or informational transmitting (e.g. considerable media protection of a terrorist assault).

Often, those suffering from a specific phobia cannot identify the key reason why their phobia developed. As the cause of a particular phobia could be unknown, it is necessary to identify the symptoms and understand that phobias could be treatable if you look for help from a mental doctor.

Risk Factors

Risk factors for creating a particular phobia are temperamental, environmental, and genetic. For example, unfavorable affectivity (a propensity to experience negative emotions such as for example disgust, anger, dread or guilt) or behavioral inhibition are temperamental risk elements for a number of anxiety disorders, including particular phobias.

Parental overprotectiveness, physical and sexual abuse, and traumatic encounters are types of environmental risk factors that boost the likelihood of a person creating a specific phobia.

There can also be a genetic susceptibility to a particular group of a particular phobia; for instance, if an individual comes with an instant relative with a particular situational phobia of flying, the average person is most likely to really have the same particular phobia than any additional group of phobia.

Symptoms of Specific Phobias

Physical Symptoms:

- Racing heart

- Difficulty breathing

- Trembling or shaking

- Sweating

- Nausea

- Dry mouth

- Chest pain or tightness

Emotional Symptoms:

- Feeling overpowering anxiety or fear

- Knowing that your dread is irrational, but sense powerless to overcome it

- Concern with losing control

- Feeling an intense have to escape

DSM-5 Diagnostic Criteria

- Marked fear or anxiety in regards to a particular object or scenario (In children fear or anxiety could be expressed simply by crying, tantrums, freezing, or clinging).

- The phobic object or situation more often than not provokes immediate fear or anxiety.

- The phobic object or situation is avoided or endured with extreme fear or anxiety.

- Worries or anxiety has gone out of proportion to

the actual danger posed by the precise object or situation and also to the sociocultural context.

- Worries, anxiety, or avoidance is persistent, typically enduring for six months or more.

- Worries, anxiety, or avoidance causes clinically significant distress or impairment in social, occupational, or other important regions of functioning.

The disturbance isn't better explained by symptoms of another mental disorder, including fear, anxiety, and avoidance of circumstances connected with panic-like symptoms or various other incapacitating symptoms; items or situations linked to obsessions; reminders of traumatic occasions; separation from your home or attachment numbers; or social situations.

Treatment Options

Like all anxiety disorders, specific phobias could be

treatable by using a mental doctor. Treatment options for particular phobias can involve therapeutic technique, medicine, or a mixture of both.

Cognitive Behavioral Therapy (CBT)

The American Psychological Association defines cognitive-behavioral therapy (CBT) as "something of treatment involving a concentrate on thinking and its own influence on both behavior and feelings." CBT emphasizes the part of dysfunctional beliefs and their impact on emotional and behavioral outcomes. The treatment targets changing such mental poison and dysfunctional beliefs to be able to change the reaction to the phobic stimulus. That is first rung on the ladder, but treatment of a particular phobia also entails gradual contact with the fear stimulus.

Medication

In some cases, a professional healthcare professional might decide that medications ought to be found in conjunction with CBT. Various kinds' of medication are accustomed to deal with phobias. A course of anti-depressants called selective serotonin reuptake inhibitors (SSRIs), such as for example Zoloft, Prozac, Celexa and others could be prescribed. Anti-anxiety medicines may also be effective in calming psychological and physical reactions to particular phobias.

CHAPTER 9

Depression and Stress in

UNIVERSITY STUDENTS: A GENUINE

Epidemic?

Are degrees of depression and anxiety actually spiking about university campuses or are college students today just better in requesting and seeking help?

Adjusting to university could be a challenge that attracts many learners and their own families by shock. Effectively navigating adult-like obligations, increased academic tension and interpersonal pressure need cognitive maturity and existence skills that lots of in this generation are still learning.

At the same time when mental health specialists, advocacy organizations and public health organizations describe the incidence of anxiety and depression among university students and college-age adults as an epidemic one, it's well worth pointing out that lots of common disorders including depression, anxiety, schizophrenia, feeling disorders, and personality disorders emerge during young adulthood. In an assessment of the books regarding the age group of starting point of mental wellness disorders, experts noted that by age 25, 75% of these who'll have a mental wellness disorder experienced their first starting point.

Many, if not most, universities and colleges report an increasing quantity of students looking for help at guidance centers, sometimes leading to difficulty maintaining the necessity for these solutions. What's behind this upsurge in demand, and will it stem from a genuine rise in mental health issues or from societal shifts that motivate and allow students to discuss a thing that used to be more taboo? *The answer, of course, is complicated.*

No two college students are exactly as well, and folks arrive on campus with a wide selection of encounters, beliefs, and worries that impact their emotional condition and also their probability of seeking help. Occasionally students enter university having been identified as having anxiety within their early teenagers or even more youthful. Sometimes a particular event through the university years because a routine of anxious convinced that can't be found in senior high school. Sometimes the reason isn't immediately apparent.

What sort of Traumatic Event Can Result in a Problem

In senior high school, Jasmine Williams taken into consideration herself someone people leaned on. "I had been always viewed as the solid friend and the 'big sister,'" says the Virginia-based 24-12 months-aged digital media professional and presenter who says she experienced no connection with anxiety. However, soon into her freshman year at High Stage University or college in High Stage, New York, Jasmine's older sibling died all of a sudden. This tragedy delivered her right into a whirlwind of stress that is making her get bewildered and drained, simply as she had a need to navigate her access into young adulthood.

But after her brother's abrupt passing, Jasmine found herself struggling to cope with change of any sort. It got so very bad that if the deadline for a paper was relocated, she would discover herself with a race heart. "I possibly could feel myself sort of spiraling," she recalls. "As the reduction was so unpredicted, I believe that forced me as I grieved to dread change, to dread the unexpected. There have been years of my entire life where I didn't even understand that stress was what I got. I just understood I experienced different."

High Point linked Jasmine with the school's emotional-support services including counseling sessions (at simply no additional expense) at the campus health center. In this difficult period, Jasmine created a kinship with additional students who had been struggling. The main element? Checking and posting her emotions with her peers rather than going right through her day time pretending everything was good.

Once she started discussing her feelings, her email inbox and mobile phone became "flooded" with communications from other people who were also coping with panic and tension. "People can't assist you to if indeed they don't understand what's heading on," she clarifies. "The earlier you let other people in, whether it's a counselor friend, the earlier you can obtain not merely empathy but alleviation."

For why so many teenagers appear to be experiencing anxiousness, stress, and depressive disorder even in the lack of acute traumatic events just like the one she suffered, Jasmine feels it has related to dread. "[It's] this overriding idea around control, I think-a feeling that everything has gone out of your control," she says adding that, "many learners are unnerved by a sense that they can't control what's arriving next."

Seeking More Help

At least one professional hesitates to label the increase of university students requesting help as a genuine mental health problems on campus. As organizations confront the cumulative effect from many years of increasing demand for mental wellness services it's vital that you remember that educational institutions actively worked well to create the demand they may be seeing now.

(The Guts for Collegiate Mental Wellness at Penn Condition is an worldwide practice-research network of almost 550 universities and colleges that works to comprehend college student mental health. CCMH gathers and analyses data on university students seeking mental wellness treatment at their educational institutions in America and internationally and publishes an annual statement. The 2018 record, the CCMH's 10th, explains the encounters of 179,964 university students seeking mental wellness treatment; 3,723 clinicians; and a lot more than 1,384,712 visits from the 2017-18 educational year.)

"During the last 15 years, the culture of society offers significantly changed," detailing that enormous amounts of money have already been spent in the last decade. On suicide consciousness you start with the youngest students-kids in primary school. "[These attempts] dramatically boost the rate of which people look for mental wellness services."

Quite simply, people who previously were feeling anxious or stressed out may have suffered alone or talked it out with family and friends, whereas now-thanks to less stigma encircling mental health issues and better-trained "gatekeepers" such as for example teachers, parents, and coaches-it's become a lot more acceptable and actually desirable to actively seek counseling.

"Students today are more ready to acknowledge any type of mental wellness concern than anytime ever sold." "This creates a notion of demand and turmoil that might not become wholly accurate." For example, records shows that 35% of the college students seeking guidance help at Penn Condition buy into the declaration: "I've thoughts of closing my entire life," at any level on the level of 0 to 4. After viewing a counselor only once, that contract drops to 9.5% of students who go to the counseling center.

Suicide prices in the higher-education establishing have remained constant or even dropped slightly in the last few years as the suicide price for the populace all together has skyrocketed. Likewise, rates of learners on anti-anxiety medicine or antidepressants possess remained flat.

What label of studies that indicate extremely high prices of stress and anxiety and major depression among the university student populace? It is asserts that they could lead visitors to believe the occurrence of the conditions is greater than for the reason that study response rates general are low, and the students who perform respond will tend to be "psychologically connected to this issue." This self-selecting band of responders may be skewing results in some instances.

Getting together with a Need

Having said that, it is recognized that mental wellness needs are actual for a considerable number of adults. The all-pervasive reach of sociable press, hyper-competition among young students, and over-included parents will surely increase stress and donate to anxiety and melancholy.

Like various other schools, Penn Condition is rising to meet up the increased demand for services by hiring even more mental doctors, keeping a 24/7 hotline staffed, and supplying a crisis text service that links students with community resources, among additional initiatives. Even though more unfiltered vocabulary students make use of today to spell out their emotional condition may heighten and also exaggerate the feeling of urgency sometimes, he explained, nobody desires to deny help a truly battling pupil: "Organizations have to react every time. The brand new demand we're viewing is not heading away."

Acknowledgments

The Glory of this book success goes to God Almighty and my beautiful Family, Fans, Readers & well-wishers, Customers and Friends for their endless support and encouragements.

www.ingramcontent.com/pod-product-compliance
Lightning Source LLC
Chambersburg PA
CBHW051036030426

42336CB00015B/2907

9781685220402